AF477552

ANGEL
BEACH
PARKING
VISIT OUR
SHOPS AND
RESTAURANTS

Main St. to Malibu

ALL-NEW PHOTO TREASURY OF CELEBRATED SCENES AND MEMORABILIA

Yesterday & Today

by Fred E. Basten

Other Books by Fred E. Basten:

Santa Monica Bay: The First 100 Years

Beverly Hills: Portrait of a Fabled City

Gringo: A Young American's Flight from Hell (with Robert Miller)

Glorious Technicolor: The Movies' Magic Rainbow

Bruin Country: A Pictorial Grand Tour of the Famed UCLA Campus

An Illustrated Guide to the Legendary Trees of Santa Monica Bay

FIRST PRINTING

Library of Congress Catalog Card Number 80-83608

Published by Graphics Press, Santa Monica, CA 90404

Photo (preceding page): Actress Natalie Wood runs along Santa Monica Pier's boardwalk in a scene from the 1965 Warner Bros. film, *Inside Daisy Clover*.

ISBN 0-937536-00-8

PRINTED IN THE UNITED STATES OF AMERICA

INTRODUCTION

In 1975, Santa Monica celebrated its 100th anniversary. The year-long centennial celebration was more than a city-wide event, however, It touched the residents of the surrounding beachside communities as well and, in doing so, activated a deep interest in the fascinating development of the entire Bay area.

If the centennial's great success proved one thing it was that the people of Santa Monica Bay were extraordinary. They truly cared about their unique surroundings. Their home was more than just the idyllic place to live.

My first book, *Santa Monica Bay: The First 100 Years*, was released just prior to the start of the centennial. It was an ambitious project, one that took several years to complete. Yet I worked filled with doubts, often wondering if the general public would be as enamored as I was with a study of local history.

I soon learned that my fears were unfounded. Shortly after the release of the book I began to receive letters not only from residents of all ages but from visitors who had seen the book during their stay. Many of these interested people expressed a personal desire to know more about a certain period of Bay area development. Others requested copies of specific stills used in the book. There were calls from students and artists, architects and designers, even local merchants. The Disney studios wanted photos to authenticate building designs of an earlier period for a film in preparation. A representative of producer Steven Spielberg needed detailed views of the early amusement piers for a sequence in his film, *1941*.

Admittedly, *Santa Monica Bay: The First 100 Years* was far from complete. Because of deadlines and space restrictions I was unable to use a number of important photos from my collection. And, in my enthusiasm to complete the book, many historical sights and scenes were overlooked.

In the few years since Santa Monica's centennial, the Bay area has been the scene of incredible progress and change. New buildings have risen to alter the skyline, forgotten lands have given way to new parklands and beaches, monuments to another time have disappeared while still others, thanks to the new awareness of our heritage, have been honored as landmarks.

These changes, and scores more, are the basis of *Main St. to Malibu*. But this book is not concerned solely with recent expansion. Much of the past has been included, too. Those never-seen photos originally intended for the earlier book are now in print. And those once over-looked subjects receive their rightful acclaim.

Main St. to Malibu is an all-new collection of photos and memorabilia and, unlike *Santa Monica Bay: The First 100 Years*, does not attempt to relate the history of the Bay area. It is, instead, a scrapbook of times past and present. If the images on these pages stir a memory or preserve a glimpse of today for tomorrow, they've accomplished my aim.

F.E.B.

(Photo opposite page) Bronze bust of Santa Monica's founder, John P. Jones, stands near the mid-point of the Third Street Mall. The parklands known today as Lincoln and Palisades Parks were among his many generous gifts to the city.

Santa Monica's oldest masonry building was designated as a landmark during the city's centennial year on August 20, 1975. A portion of its colorful past is noted on the plaque that now adorns the facade. It states, in part, "This building . . . was erected in October, 1875, as a tavern by William Rapp. Known as Rapp's Saloon, it served as the town hall from May, 1887, to January, 1889." The historic structure is located at 1438 Second Street.

Entrance to Santa Monica Canyon, 1884. The dirt road leading up from the Pavilion (center) is today's Chautauqua Boulevard.

Santa Monica's palisades have been a scenic wonder for centuries — and an obstacle to beachgoers for nearly as long. By the 1880s, stairs had become a vital link to the shore. They remain a much-used and practical means to this day.

Another view of the famous "99 steps," looking south toward the steepled Arcadia Hotel near Railroad Avenue, now Colorado (today's Arcadia Terrace more accurately marks the hotel site).

The original "99 steps" led from the palisades at the foot of Arizona Avenue to the beachlands below, ca 1889.

With the installation of railroad tracks at the base of the palisades the original "99 steps" had to be removed and a longer stairway, one that allowed trains to pass underneath, was built in its place. This structure became the forerunner of the overpasses that bridge today's Pacific Coast Highway.

"55 steps," another busy access to the beach, descended from the palisades at the foot of Railroad Avenue. The tunnel provided entrance to the shoreline for trains traveling up the coast to the once thriving "Port of Los Angeles." Since widened and named McClure Tunnel, it is today the heavily traveled entrance to the Santa Monica Freeway.

Ascending this dizzying stairway, non-stop, provides a real test even for the sturdiest legs. It connects Adelaide Drive above with the crossroads of Ocean Avenue, Entrada Drive and Channel Road in Santa Monica Canyon below, 1979.

Until 1978, the only route for beachgoers down the hillside at the foot of Montana Avenue was a treacherous footpath. In 1979, a winding stairway was completed and opened to the public, only to be washed out during the damaging winter rains of January, 1980. The overpass (right) is one of three new spans built during 1978-79. (Construction of a high-rise beach facility, the Gables Club, was begun at the base of the palisades in the 1920s but abandoned following the stock market crash of 1929. Most of the ruins were removed in the mid-70s and the remaining walls decorated with murals.)

Artist's rendering of Port Ballona, proposed town and harbor on the salt marshes and lagoons mid-way between Santa Monica and Playa del Rey, 1887. The two piers were under construction when the project was discontinued for lack of funds. The concept was 70 years ahead of its time. Today, the area is the site of the Marina del Rey harbor and channel.

"In 1893, the Southern Pacific Railroad Company completed its 4,720-foot wharf which served as a deep water port for the Los Angeles area. After San Pedro became Los Angeles' official harbor in 1897, shipping activity at Port Los Angeles declined. Ultimately abandoned and dismantled, no trace remains of what had been the longest wooden pier in the world." So reads the plaque set in a boulder at the site of the Long Wharf, between water's edge and Pacific Coast Highway opposite Potrero Canyon. Designated as a California Historical Landmark on July 13, 1976.

Southern Pacific excursion trains pull into the Santa Monica depot, 1892. The small hotel at the corner of Railroad and Ocean Avenues (right center), with its banner touting "the cheapest and best meals for 25¢," will become the prestigious Santa Monica Hotel before the end of the decade.

By 1900, shipping activity at Port Los Angeles had dwindled to such a point that sightseers accounted for the greatest activity — and the once-busy railroad tracks along the base of Santa Monica's palisades showed the effects as beach brush began to grow unchallenged.

The new Santa Monica Hotel, ca 1898, offered everchanging view of the nearby train depot from its broad veranda. Among the hotel's competitors were the beachfront Arcadia, just to the west, and the Hotel Ross (photo right) which claimed to be "the cheapest and best place in town."

HOTEL
HOTEL ROSS
CHEAPEST & BEST PLACE IN TOWN. MEALS
DINING ROOM
OFFICE

The intersection of Oregon Street (now Santa Monica Boulevard) and Third Street, late 1890s. The corner building housed the Bank of Santa Monica and the town's first library.

The popular Third Street trolley offered local service to Santa Monica commuters, ca 1898. Streetcars also traveled San Vicente, Santa Monica and Lincoln Boulevards, Broadway, Ocean and Montana Avenues (the Ocean Avenue car traveled southward along the present Neilson Way and Pacific Street to Venice, Playa del Rey and more distant South Bay communities) and, for a time after the steam trains to the Long Wharf stopped running, along the beach.

The magnificent Moreton Bay fig tree (*Ficus Macrophylla*) on the grounds of the Miramar Hotel is one of Santa Monica's oldest and most famous landmarks. Planted in 1879 by John P. Jones, the city's founder, it is the sole reminder of his elegant estate, Miramar, that once covered the square block area bounded by Ocean and California Avenues, Wilshire Boulevard and Second Street.

Fashionable houses line Ocean Avenue in this view looking north from Oregon Street (Santa Monica Boulevard), ca 1900. Even today, sidewalks along this picturesque stretch remain wider than normal to accommodate strollers.

D. E. Fletcher, one of "faraway" Topanga Canyon's earliest merchants, stands at the doorway to his general store, The Outside Inn, ca 1900. Aside from offering gas and oil, tobacco products, ice cold drinks and groceries for motorists, the establishment rented tent houses, complete with running water, for light housekeeping.

Zuma Beach (below), once a muddy catch-basin for the swampy lowlands of Ramirez Canyon, is today one of Southern California's most popular oceanside playgrounds. (Right) Three visitors to Malibu's sprawling Rindge Ranch ride a flat car over the railroad trestle spanning the Ramirez Canyon gorge, early 1900s.

Ocean Park's Main Street, looking north from Pier Avenue, 1901.

Visitors stroll along the boardwalk while others relax under umbrellas on the sand at Santa Monica's North Beach Bath House, ca 1900.

2612

Historic residence of Roy Jones, son of Santa Monica's founder, was moved from its original site in the 1000 block of Ocean Avenue to the corner of Main Street and Ocean Park Boulevard in March, 1977. The Victorian-style home was fully restored for official opening in October, 1980, as Heritage Square Museum (far left). Smaller photo shows the Jones home as it appeared at the turn of the century.

The canals of Venice, patterned after those of the town's namesake in Italy, were the inspiration of wealthy manufacturer and promoter, Abbot Kinney. The entire excavation project was accomplished during the summer of 1904 but few of the waterways remain today. Most were filled and paved as streets in 1927.

Tea gardens, cafes, curio shops, even real estate offices helped attract crowds to bustling Pier Avenue in Ocean Park, 1905.

A walk through Palisades Park, with its sweeping ocean view, was a favorite pastime with residents and visitors alike even in 1905. Today, the 14-block-long strip attracts large numbers of joggers as well.

Windward Avenue, looking west to the entrance of the Venice Pier, from Pacific Circle, 1908. To help promote Venice, Abbot Kinney once imported camels for rides, and built a miniature train to take passengers on a tour of the community.

Looking east along Windward Avenue. Venice's famous main street earned the title "Road to a Thousand Wonders."

Santa Monica's Third Street on a gray winter day, 1907, looking north from the Utah (now Broadway) intersection. The corner building (right) housed a second floor auditorium known as Steere's Opera House.

The mosque-like Ocean Park Bath House, built by developer A.R. Fraser, offered indoor and outdoor swimming for year-round enjoyment, 1910.

Ocean Front Walk, looking south toward Fraser's Pier, 1910.

Fraser's Million Dollar Pier, taken from the roof of the nearby Ocean Park Bath House, 1910. Angelotti's Hungarian Orchestra was appearing at the huge over-the-water auditorium (left) while, at the pier's entrace, the Starland Theater featured vaudeville.

5516.

Municipal Pier, ca 1915. The original concrete pilings were replaced with wood in 1920 when salt water rusted the reinforcing steel, causing the concrete to shatter.

Horse-drawn wagons haul supplies to construction site of Santa Monica's Municipal Pier, ca 1912.

The building that houses today's Mayfair Music Hall at 214 Santa Monica Boulevard was built in 1911 as a legitimate theater. The venture was not to last. Within several years it was converted to a "motion picture house" and, as the Majestic Theater, gained its early fame.

(Right) Souvenir menu presented to "Race Divers, Friends of the Newspapers and Race Officials" of the 1915 Venice Grand Prix. The luncheon was held at the Ship Cafe on Venice Pier; a short distance from the beachfront road, Speedway, named after the once-annual event. (Below) Santa Monica, too, had its road races as seen in this 1912 shot taken near the Ocean Avenue grandstands. Many great drivers of the day, including Barney Oldfield and Ralph de Palma, took part in the pre-World War I competition.

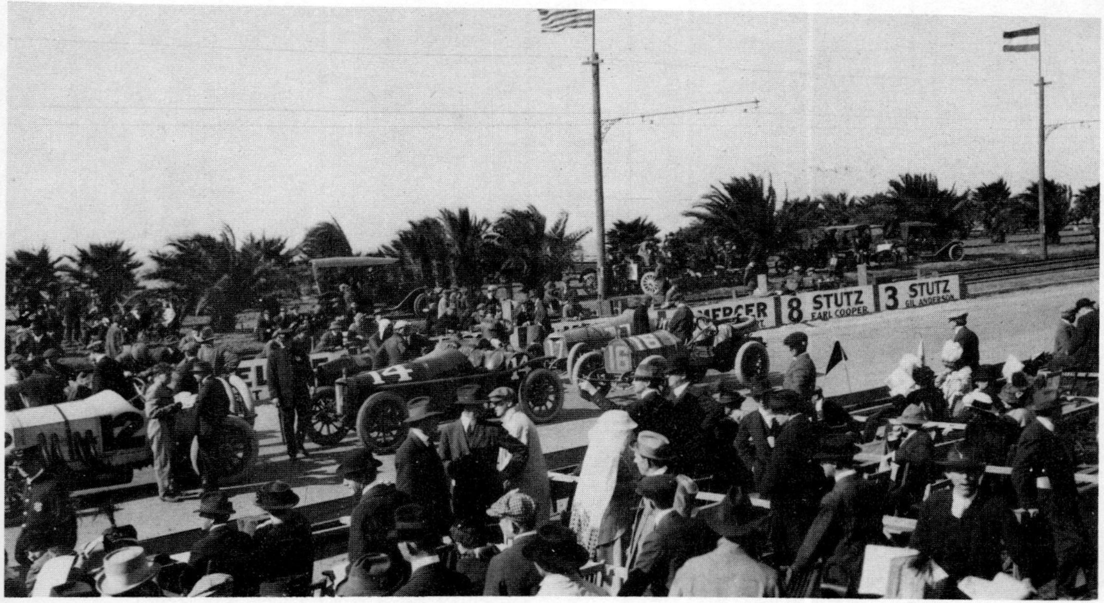

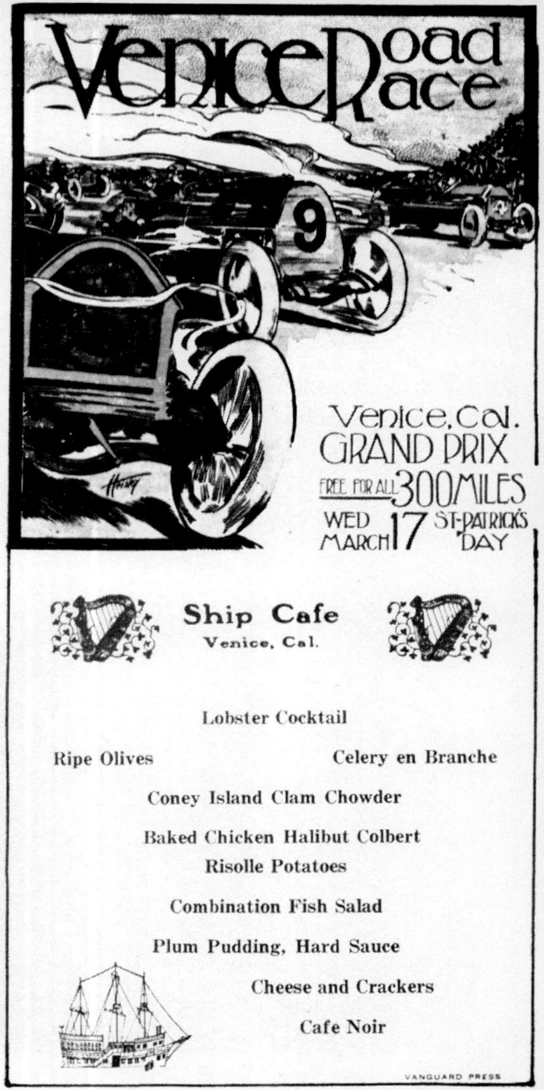

Ship Cafe
Venice, Cal.

Lobster Cocktail

Ripe Olives — Celery en Branche

Coney Island Clam Chowder

Baked Chicken Halibut Colbert
Risolle Potatoes

Combination Fish Salad

Plum Pudding, Hard Sauce

Cheese and Crackers

Cafe Noir

VANGUARD PRESS

World-famous Venice Beach, with its huge indoor plunge (far right), attracted visitors from near and far. Photo was taken from the Venice Pier, 1918.

Villa City, furnished, rental cottages along a Venice canal, as it looked in 1918. Many of the units remain today (inset).

Snapshots taken at Venice Pier's Ship Cafe, a gathering place for the "in" crowd of the day, were treasured mementos.

Mack Sennett's bathing beauties were frequently seen frolicking along the local beaches. Here, between scenes of the 1918 comedy, *Whose Little Wife Are You?* The Bay area continues to be a favorite locale for motion picture and, now, television productions.

The old Ocean Park fire house, a reminder of earlier days, still stands at the corner of Rose Avenue and Main Street.

Santa Monica Bay as seen from the rustic-railed California Avenue incline, 1918. Before the roadway was widened and graded it was known as the Sunset Trail.

Hotel Cadillac
EVERY MODERN CONVENIENCE
B. F. & M. S. GREEN, PROPS.
B. F. GREEN, MGR.
OCEAN FRONT AT DUDLEY
VENICE, CALIFORNIA
PHONE 63165
Unobstructed View of the Pacific and
Wonderful Sunsets

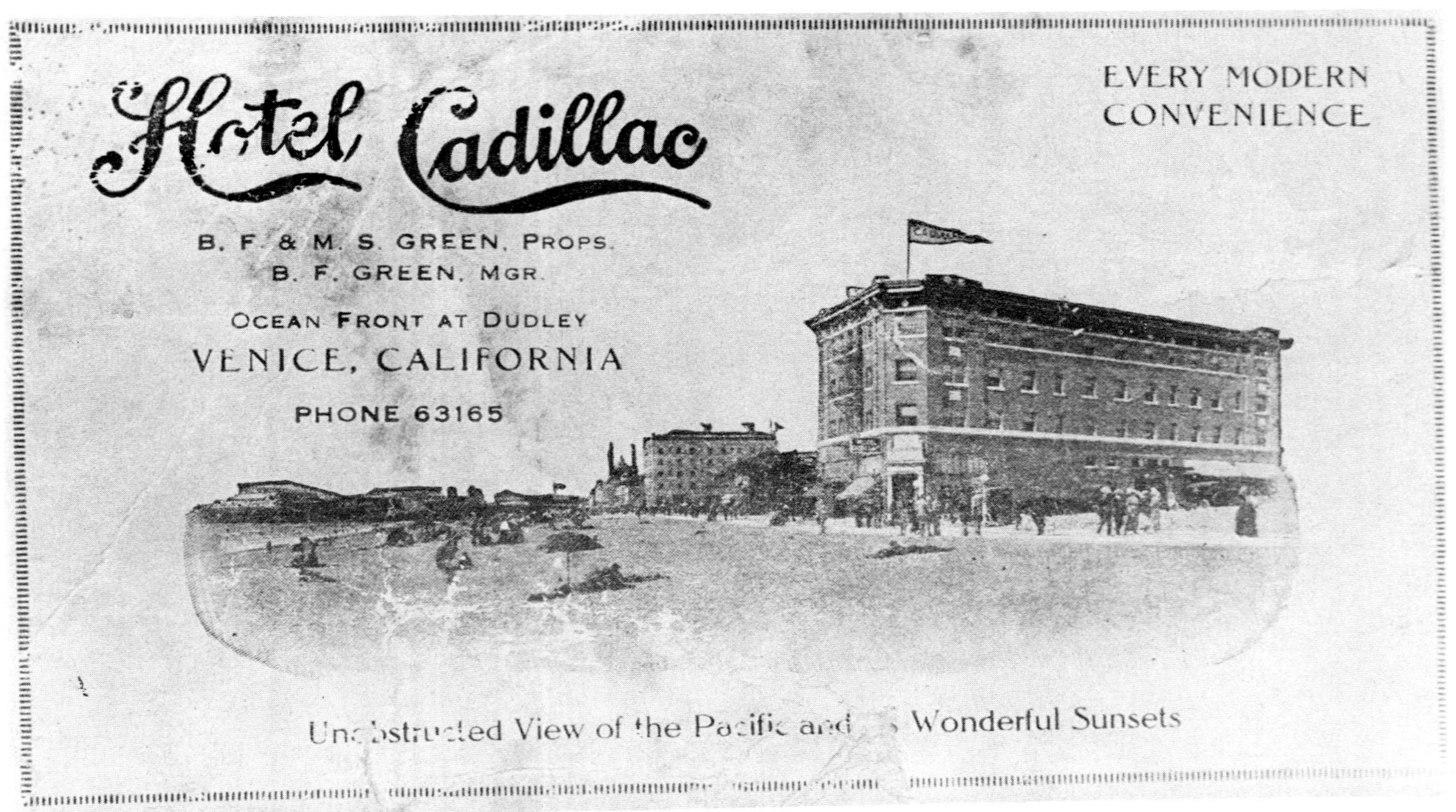

Ad from 1920.

Auditorium, Venice Pier, 1920. The Ship Cafe is barely visible at right.

TOPANGA CANYON, CAL.

Traveling south on the beach road between today's Coastline Drive and Porto Marina Way in Pacific Palisades, ca 1919. Castle Rock, the pinnacle-shaped formation, was removed prior to widening the highway.

Car pauses along dirt roadway to let driver and passengers get a closer look at Topanga Canyon's first highway bridge, ca 1920.

Since the mid-1920's, the monumental structure rising from the Castellammare hillside (above) overlooking Pacific Coast Highway has intrigued passersby. Often referred to as "the castle," the huge estate built by Russian-born Lazare Kaufman has been the source of many rumors, the most widespread (and inaccurate) naming it the royal home for Prince Ali Kahn and Rita Hayworth after their marriage in 1949. Malibu, too, has its mountain castle — a turreted medieval-style structure that began rising above the Civic Center in the mid-1970s. It was listed on the market in 1980 for $5.5 million.

The sprawling Spanish-style building at the overpass on Pacific Coast Highway in Pacific Palisades was built in the 1920s as a community center for the then new Castellammare development on the hillside above the beach. But it was as Thelma Todd's Sidewalk Cafe — a posh restaurant, gambling casino and hideaway — that it gained world-wide attention. In December of 1935, the angel-faced film actress was found dead in her chocolate-colored Phaeton, wearing a $20,000 mink coat and a fortune in jewels, in a garage just up the road. Did she die of natural causes? Was it murder — or suicide? The events leading to Thelma Todd's death remain a mystery to this day.

Santa Monica beach, railroad tracks still intact, looking north from the palisades at the California Avenue incline, 1923.

Today's Douglas Park on Wilshire Boulevard between Chelsea and 25th Streets was the site of an abandoned movie studio when Donald W. Douglas and a small group of associates selected it as the initial location for the Douglas Aircraft Company in 1922. The Wilshire plant was to remain active through 1928 when Douglas purchased land adjacent to Clover Field Airport. Charles Lindbergh's landing and takeoff from the old Douglas Field in 1927 was the last from the site.

Sunny days drew large crowds to popular Ocean Park beach, early 1920s. At night, the throngs moved indoors to dance in the cavernous ballrooms along the beach fronts and on the piers.

Main entrance to the Egyptian Ballroom in Ocean Park.

Dance

At the

RENDEZVOUS Ball Room

CRYSTAL BEACH

Foot of Strand Street

SANTA MONICA

Private parties, large and small given special attention

Ad from 1924.

Ornate interior of the La Monica Ballroom on Santa Monica Pier, 1924. With a capacity for 10,000 persons, it is said to have been the world's largest dance arena of its kind.

(Right) Ad from 1924

Don Clark and his La Monica Orchestra

Dancing Every Night in the Year

Evenings at 7:30 - Usual Matinees 2:30

Loge Seat Reservations - Phone 24965

SANTA MONICA PIER AT COLORADO AVE.

In the 1920s, a young Venice High School student posed for a statue to adorn the grassy main entry to the campus. The girl became famous as Myrna Loy, the actress; the statue became a Venice landmark. For over 50 years, the work by sculptor Harry Sinebrenner went unharmed, except for coats of paint applied by football rivals. In 1979, vandals destroyed not only the graceful Loy likeness but the flanking pieces. Restoration began in Spring of 1980.

Proposed Santa Monica breakwater, 1926, an elaborate plan that was eventually dropped in favor of a more modest one. With growing interest in yachting and boating, despite the Great Depression, a bond issue was passed to build a breakwater opposite the end of Municipal Pier. The first attempt was a disaster and the tied concrete caisons, set into sandbars, broke away in the heavy currents. In 1933, construction on a 2,000-foot rock breakwater was begun. Again, heavy seas won out, ripping away the upper portion so that today only a portion is visible at high tide. The remaining breakwater's only benefit, over the years, has been to change the natural sand-carrying currents in the area, thus greatly widening the beach.

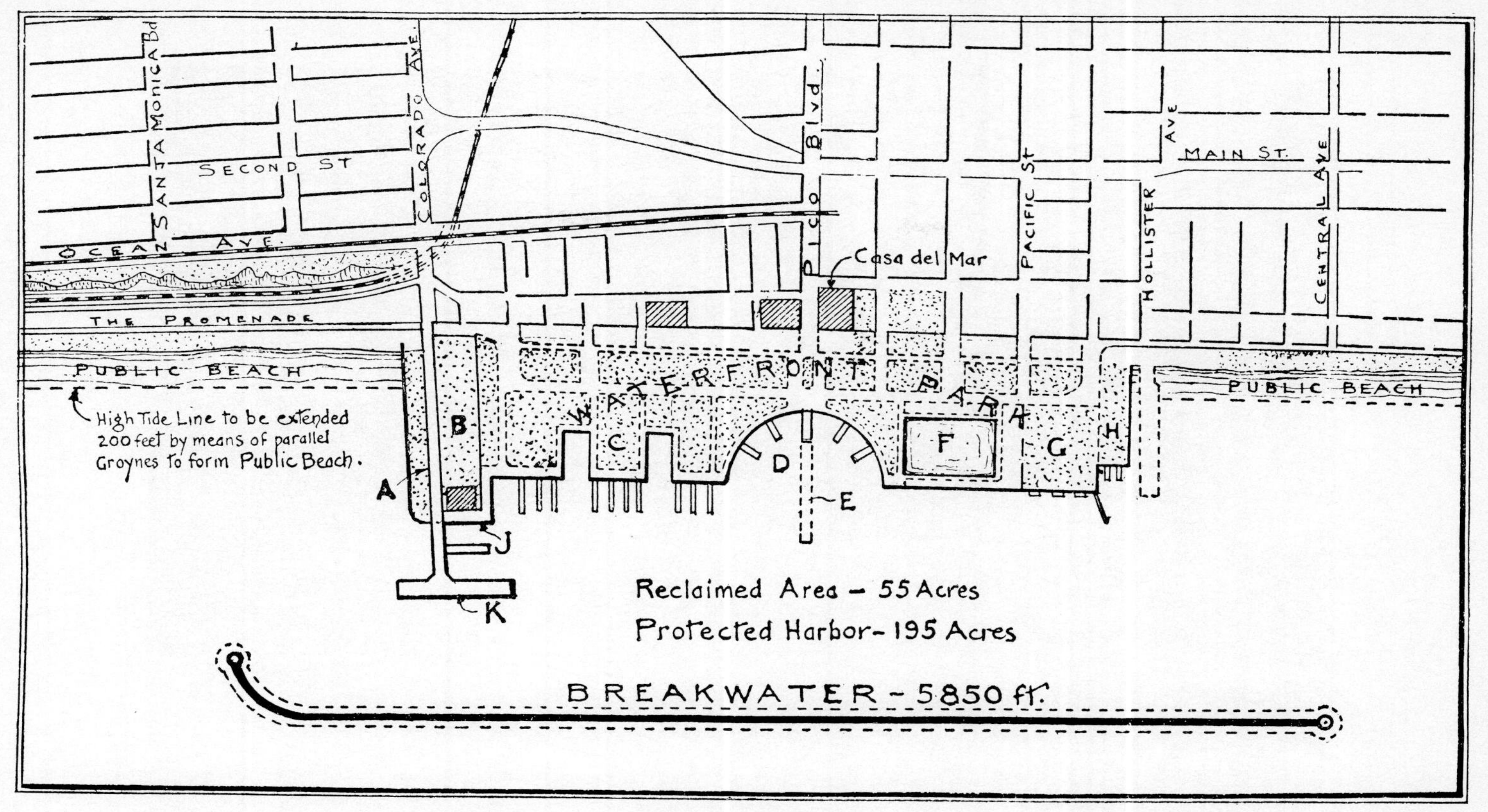

Proposed Break Water

A—Municipal Pier
B—Amusements
C—Yacht Clubs
D—Small Boat Harbor
E—Pier Franchises

F—Open Air Swimming Pool
G—U. S. Sea Plane Base
H—Marine Way and Yacht Repair
J—Fishing Harbor
K—Steamship Pier

Guarded entrance to the famed Malibu Colony. In 1926, Anna Q. Nillson, of silent movie fame, moved to this private beachfront area and started the celebrity invasion.

In 1924, wealthy Adolph Bernheimer purchased seven-plus acres on a mesa overlooking the ocean in Pacific Palisades. For three years, crews worked to transform the former mule camp, a housing site for men and equipment used in the construction of local roadways, into one of the most magnificent gardens in the world. Bernheimer Oriental Gardens attracted an average of 5,000 visitors a week to view its elaborate temples, pagodas (one a huge bronze copy of its famous original in China), ancient art objects, waterfalls and ponds set among massive planting of fushias, begonias and lotus blossoms. In 1948, a landslide forced closing of the property. Above, the impressive entrance to the gardens, 1929. Right, a lone wall paralleling Sunset Boulevard near Marquez Place is all that remains today.

The Bliss Building at Fifth Street and Santa Monica Boulevard, 1928.

Guests relax in the secluded gardens of the Miramar Hotel, 1928.

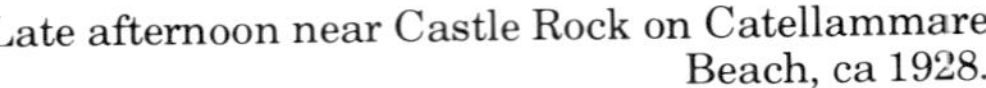

Late afternoon near Castle Rock on Catellammare Beach, ca 1928.

Santa Monica College, formally established as a junior college in 1929, was originally housed in a few upstairs rooms of the high school at Seventh Street and Michigan Avenue. In 1945, the city's adult education program, the old Santa Monica Technical School and the junior college were merged and, eight years later, these divisions were eliminated allowing the college to function administratively as a unified institution. Today, Santa Monica College is located on 45 acres fronting Pico Boulevard between 16th and 22 Streets. (Left) The modernistic clock tower, a campus landmark.

Santa Monica Municipal Golf Course and Club House at Clover Field, 1928.

Beach Club logo, 1928.

Fishing off Santa Monica Municipal Pier, ca 1930.

Santa Monica's famed amusement area, 1929. The roller coaster was the main attraction on today's Newcomb Pier (earlier Loof Pier) while the major buildings, topped with domes, lined Municipal Pier.

In its 50-plus years of operation, the pier's famous merry-go-round has been seen in many films (here, on the set of *The Sting*, 1973). The carousel features 46 handmade horses imported from Germany and the oldest organ in the country, built in 1900 by the Wurlitzer Company.

GAS
CASH GROCERY
SANDWICHES
GROCERIES
SODA
Ballantynes

A winter's day at the beach. Cars fill the parking lots and streets around Santa Monica Canyon on February 28, 1932, to take advantage of the bright sun and calm surf. Looking south from Huntington Palisades.

Santa Monica's Main Street city hall opened in 1938 on property acquired from the Southern Pacific Railway Company. The new facility, with its spacious Art Deco-tiled lobby, replaced the older quarters then located at the northwest corner of Fourth Street and Santa Monica Boulevard.

Headquarters for Associated Telephone Company (now General Telephone) at 155 Marine Street — now Barnard Way, just west of Neilson Way, in Ocean Park. Used today as a switching station, the building's appearance, with its filled in windows and main entry, has changed considerably since the early 1930s. At that time, Bank of Ocean Park had the corner location.

ASSOCIATED TELEPHONE COMPANY, LTD.
ASSOCIATED TELEPHONE COMPANY, LTD.

Topanga Creek passes under Roosevelt Highway (now Pacific Coast Highway) bridge on its way into the bay, mid-1930s. Looking south toward auto camp and, in the distance, the mountain plateau that is now Sunset Mesa.

Throngs of applicants line up for work at Douglas Aircraft plant in Santa Monica, 1939. Climbing orders for military planes and a boom in civilian aviation spurred employment.

Searchlights and anti-aircraft guns comb the sky for unseen enemy over Bay area on February 25, 1942. Photo, snapped during a wartime blackout, clearly shows blobs of light made by exploding shells.

Marker commemorating the 400th anniversary of the founding of Santa Monica Bay by Juan Cabrillo on October 8, 1542, stands in Palisades Park at the foot of California Avenue.

Ocean Park Boulevard teams with war workers changing shifts at nearby Douglas plant, 1942. At the height of the war, the huge factory was camouflaged with over 4.5 million feet of net. Fake houses, gardens and trees, with employees tending them, were constructed on the roof to blend in with the surrounding subdivisions. The Douglas operation was used as a model for other war plants and hailed as the finest example of protective obscurement in the world.

The Olympic Drive-In Theater, on the eastern edge of Santa Monica (northwest corner of Olympic Boulevard and Bundy Drive), was Southern California's first outdoor movie house and only the second built in the United States. It was in operation from 1946 through the early 1970s.

In 1926, actress Marion Davies announced plans to build a beach house in Santa Monica. Four years later, at a cost of nearly $2 million, her storybook Georgian-style mansion (55 bathrooms, 37 fireplaces) was completed. In the years Miss Davies lived there, she spent another $4 million on furnishings and "improvements," only to sell the property in 1945 for $600,000. In 1949, the mansion was remodeled as a lavish hotel (Ocean House) and opened to the public. By 1960, the colonnaded main house, with its Tiffany chandeliers and 300-year-old marble mantles, had been leveled for a parking lot. The Italian marble swimming pool, cabanas and guest house remain today, used by members of a private club.

(Left) Looking west along Santa Monica Boulevard from 20th Street, 1964. (Above) Plaque in Palisades Park at the terminal end of "the Main Street of America," Route 66 (Santa Monica Boulevard).

Looking south along an old Venice canal, 1950s. Oil shortages of the 1970s revived interests in drilling, only this time offshore within the bay.

(Far left) Saint John's Hospital and surrounding area, 1955. Santa Monica Boulevard runs across bottom of photo (Left) In 1979, 22nd Street, from Arizona Avenue to Santa Monica Boulevard, was closed to through traffic and became part of Saint John's Hospital and Health Center's new forecourt.

Ocean Front Walk, looking north from Windward Avenue, 1957. *Slattery's Hurricane* was playing at the Venice Theater.

KRESS
Motherhood
MATERNITY SHOPS
SHOES
COFFEE SHOP
MATERNITY
EMPORIUM
KARLS
SHOES
SEIGEL'S
BAKERY
BAKERY
EUROPA
EUROPA CO.
SALE

The new Venice Pier, at the foot of Washington Boulevard, was officially dedicated on February 27, 1965. The old pier, off Windward Avenue, was removed in 1946.

Third Street in Santa Monica, looking south from near Wilshire Boulevard, 1965.

Santa Monica's Main Library opened in new quarters in 1965, one block east of its earlier home at Fifth Street and Santa Monica Boulevard. The Main Library and its three city branches contain nearly 330,000 books in its adult and juvenile collections plus holdings that include government documents, pamphlets, recordings and films.

The Malibu Civic Center, with its dramatic colonnade, houses the Malibu Justice Court, Branch Library, Administrative and Emergency Housing Offices. The building opened in Spring, 1970.

Santa Monica's Third Street Mall opened to great fanfare in 1965. Here, looking north from Arizona Avenue in 1968.

The marshlands of La Ballona had been favored hunting grounds from early Indian days to modern times. The last of the duck blinds were still standing in 1957 when dredging began for the Marina del Rey, and on April 10, 1965, it was officially dedicated. Today, the Marina, with nearly 6,000 recreational boat slips and surrounding restaurants, shopping centers, highrise condominiums and apartments, is recognized as the world's largest small craft harbor.

Multi-story addition, and main entry to Santa Monica Hospital, was first opened in 1969. The final phase was completed in 1974.

(Below) Lighthouse on the point opposite Potrero Canyon was once used as a lookout for mariners and, later, county lifeguards. It stood for 60 years, from 1912 to 1972. (Right) Secluded beach surrounding mouth of Topanga Creek, 1975. Removal of the houses, on state property, began in the mid-70s, opening the beach to the public.

The high curving walls of the Venice Pavilion, on the beach at Windward Avenue (the former entryway to the Venice Pier), surround a large central core that includes space for picnics, sunning and recreational activities. The Pavilion opened in the early 1960s.

VENICE PAVILION
PICNIC AREA & MURALS

With the opening of Temescal Canyon, from Sunset Boulevard to Pacific Coast Highway, to through traffic in the early 1970s drivers received another bonus. Surrounding a long portion of the winding roadway, a scenic parkland was created, complete with trails and semi-enclosed picnic grounds.

Damaged, abandoned P.O.P. amusement pier and faded storefronts along Ocean Front Walk, 1974, are reminders of another era when crowds jammed the once popular fun zone. The area was cleared several years later, providing an uninterrupted sweep of beach.

SANTA MONICA
COUNTY
BUILDING

The rolling hills overlooking Malibu's Civic Center and famed Colony were transformed in the early 1970s as construction began on the architecturally striking campus of Pepperdine University.

Construction on the original central section of Santa Monica's County Building, on the grassy slope adjacent to City Hall, began in 1950. Shortly after, the north wing was added. In 1964, the larger south wing was dedicated.

General Telephone Company headquarters, reaching 21 stories skyward at Wilshire Boulevard's westward terminal, became a new Santa Monica landmark in the early 1970s. Each Christmas Eve, the tower is transformed into a cross of lights, visible for many miles in all directions.

Lush, shaded glens, half-moon bridges, temples and meandering streams add to the tranquil setting of Pacific Palisades' Lake Shrine.

The new J. Paul Getty Museum in Pacific Palisades, opened in 1974, is a faithful recreation of the Villa dei Papiri, an ancient Roman country house buried by volcanic mud in the A.D. 79 eruption of Mount Vesuvius. Built to house the oil billionaire's extensive collection of art treasures, the museum boasts such works of major significance as a 2,300-year-old life-size Greek statue of an Olympic athlete. Attributed to the sculptor Lysippus and now called the Getty Bronze, it was purchased for a record price of $4 million.

Santa Monica Civic Auditorium, home of the Academy Awards presentations during the 1960s, is today one of the Southland's most active spots for concerts and exhibitions.

Intricate wooden arbor in Palisades Park, opposite the 900 block on Ocean Avenue, is an enduring example of turn-of-the-century craftmanship and design.

KELLAR

Starting in the 1970s, Ocean Park's Main Street experienced a renaissance, spurred by a contemporary spirit and an influx of new business. Adding to the existing creative climate were an array of distinctive antique and specialty shops, art galleries and uniquely themed restaurants.

The Bay area's two Inspiration Points: (left) the wooded northerly tip of Santa Monica's Palisades Park and (right) the lesser known but equally spectacular viewpoint at the juncture of Via de las Olas and Mount Holyoke Avenue in Pacific Palisades.

THE POINT
IS FOR YOU
TO ENJOY
DONT
LITTER

During the 1970s, Venice and roller skating became synonymous. By 1980, the beachside community had become the skating capital of the world.

Famed Serra Retreat on Malibu's Laudamus (Latin for "We Praise") Hill was reopened in early 1974 after the disastrous fire of 1970 leveled all but a portion of the historic property. The new facility, designed in the Mediterranean style of the original building, accommodates visitors, individuals and groups, from all faiths for weekend retreats.

SKATES
SKATE
SALES
RENTALS
FAMILY
RENTALS

Spirit of St. Louis
"DC" COMMERCIAL AIRLINERS SINCE 1933
McDONNELL DOUGLAS

In the late 1970s, the open spaces south of Malibu's Civic Center, once planted with acres of commercially grown flowers, began disappearing as new shops and offices were added to the busy Shopping Center.

The Donald Douglas Museum and Library opened in its present quarters at Santa Monica Airport (formerly Clover Field) on February 17, 1979. Among the more than 20,000 historic items on display are engines from early aircraft, scale models, dramatic aerospace photos, murals and charts, as well as prized mementos from the personal collections of many aviation pioneers. The suspended craft in the huge Exhibit Hall South (left photo) is a scale replica of the "Spirit of St. Louis."

One of Malibu's most publicized landslides occurred April 14, 1979, in the Big Rock area when tons of earth and rock rumbled onto Pacific Coast Highway. Unstable conditions prompted the building of an immense "wall" of steel and wood girders to protect motorists and nearby homes. By mid-June, 1980, the slide area had been sloped and covered with a massive wire net and the famous barrier removed.

Business Park, a $60 million development fronting Ocean Park Boulevard between 28th and 31st Streets, began taking shape during the late 1970s on the 57-acre site formerly occupied by Douglas Aircraft Company. The sprawling complex includes both commercial and industrial buildings.

al's & Phar

A new expression in decorative arts was born in the Venice-Ocean Park area of the 1960s. Over the next decade, wall murals of the beachfront communities began receiving deserved attention. Here, three varied and prime examples.

Groundbreaking ceremonies for First Federal Square, a new 12-story office complex, took place in July, 1979. The prismatic-shaped Main Tower, set back from Wilshire Boulevard (between Fourth and Fifth Streets) by a progressive step-back of floors, slopes up from the landscaped ground level Plaza.

The Wilshire Palisades Building, an 11-story office development overlooking Palisades Park, is the final phase of the Lawrence Welk Plaza at the foot of Wilshire Boulevard. The unique parallelogram shape of the terraced structure began rising soon after groundbreaking in September, 1979.

Robinsons

With Ronald Reagan's presidential nomination in July, 1980, his Pacific Palisades home of over 20 years became a major center of interest.

Santa Monica Place, dramatic new three-level shopping mall covering two city blocks, consists of over 150 shops, services and restaurants, two major department stores, park-like courts and pedestrian walkways with fountains, pools and plantings of trees, shrubs and flowers. The huge center opened in late 1980.

Photo credits: Bob Board, 80; First Federal Square, 116; Wilshire Palisades Bldg., 117; Santa Monica Place, 118. All other photos from the author's collection.

Saint Monica Statue.

ACKNOWLEDGMENTS

Sincere thanks to Aubrey Austin, Bob Board, Max Buckner, Dona Carn, George Dillon, Joann Duray Johnson, Mary Light, Evelyn Mount, Robert Osborne, Liz Roberson, Neil Van Scoten, Murray L. Tanner and Joe Walling for their generous help in preparing this book — and to the dedicated Reference Department staffs of the Santa Monica, Malibu, Venice and Pacific Palisades libraries for their invaluable assistance in locating factual data.

And special thanks to a very special person — Jeanne Basten, my mother — for her wonderful support and enthusiasm.

Fred E. Basten

INDEX

Sunday in Palisades Park.